Usborne Talk

HOW M...

MONKEYS?

Heather Amery
Illustrated by Malcolm Livingstone

Consultant: Betty Root
Centre for the Teaching of Reading
University of Reading, England

Old Pedro is taking lots of monkeys to the zoo.
What has happened to his truck?

The monkeys are very hot, hungry and sad.
How many can you see?

Clever Peepo has opened the door of the cage.
What are the monkeys doing?

Where is Old Pedro?
How many monkeys can you see now?

The monkeys are happy now.
How many other animals are in the picture?

Old Pedro is hot and very cross.
How many monkeys can you see?

The monkeys are playing in the trees.
Who is eating the oranges?

What are all the people doing?
How many monkeys now?

The people have seen the monkeys.
What is happening to them all?

The monkeys and their friends run away.
How many monkeys can you see?

The monkeys run into the farmyard?
Which ones are being naughty?

What other birds and animals can you see?
How many animals can you count altogether?

The horse runs away with the cart.
What other animals are running too?

Will the people catch the monkeys?
How many monkeys can you see?

The horse runs much faster than the people.
How many monkeys escaped on the cart?

First published in 1985
Usborne Publishing Ltd
20 Garrick St, London
WC2 9BJ, England
© Usborne Publishing Ltd 1985

The name of Usborne and the
device 🐝 are Trade Marks of
Usborne Publishing Ltd.

Printed in Portugal